# American Holidays
# INDEPENDENCE DAY

Connor Dayton

**PowerKiDS**
press™
New York

Published in 2012 by The Rosen Publishing Group, Inc.
29 East 21st Street, New York, NY 10010

First Edition

Editor: Jennifer Way
Book Design: Julio Gil

Photo Credits: Cover, pp. 13, 17, 20–21, 23, 24 (top left, bottom left, top right) Shutterstock.com; pp. 4–5 Ariel Skelley/Photographer's Choice/Getty Images; p. 7 SuperStock/Getty Images; p. 9 Chip Somodevilla/Getty Images; p. 11 Ariel Skelley/The Image Bank/Getty Images; p. 15 Jupiterimages/FoodPix/Getty Images; pp. 18–19, 24 (bottom right) redswept/Shutterstock.com.

Library of Congress Cataloging-in-Publication Data

Dayton, Connor.
 Independence Day / by Connor Dayton. — 1st ed.
     p. cm. — (American holidays)
 Includes index.
 ISBN 978-1-4488-6140-8 (library binding) — ISBN 978-1-4488-6238-2 (pbk.) —
ISBN 978-1-4488-6239-9 (6-pack)
 1. Fourth of July—Juvenile literature. 2. Fourth of July celebrations—Juvenile literature. I. Title.
 E286.A1263 2012
 394.2634—dc23

                         2011020569

Manufactured in the United States of America

CPSIA Compliance Information: Batch #WW12PK: For Further Information contact Rosen Publishing, New York, New York at 1-800-237-9932

# Contents

July 4 is Independence Day. It honors the 13 American colonies becoming the United States.

The **Declaration of Independence** was adopted on July 4, 1776.

Thomas Jefferson wrote the Declaration of Independence.

WE HOLD THESE TRUTHS TO BE
EVIDENT: THAT ALL MEN ARE C
EQUAL. THAT THEY ARE ENDOWED
CREATOR WITH CERTAIN INAL
RIGHTS. AMONG THESE ARE LIFE
AND THE PURSUIT OF HAPPIN
TO SECURE THESE RIGHTS GOVE
ARE INSTITUTED AMONG M
SOLEMNLY PUBLISH AND DEC
THESE COLONIES ARE AND
OUGHT TO BE FREE AND IND
STATES---AND FOR THE SUPP
DECLARATION. WITH A FIR
ON THE PROTECTION
PROVIDENCE. WE MUTUA
OUR LIVES

Americans honor Independence Day in lots of ways.

Families get together for picnics and cookouts. Cookouts are also called **barbecues**.

Some people eat apple pie on Independence Day. Washington is the state that grows the most apples.

Corn is another food eaten on this holiday. Iowa is the state that grows the most corn.

Cities have **parades** on Independence Day. The national parade is held in Washington, D.C.

19

People carry flags and wear red, white, and blue.

There are **fireworks** shows at night. This is a fun way to end America's birthday!

# Words to Know

barbecue

Declaration of Independence

fireworks

parade

## Index

## Web Sites

Due to the changing nature of Internet links, PowerKids Press has developed an online list of Web sites related to the subject of this book. This site is updated regularly. Please use this link to access the list:
www.powerkidslinks.com/amh/indepen/

24